T0194188

108

THE STORY OF DISCOVERING
EARTH'S CONSCIOUSNESS

ERIC LEO

authorHOUSE®

AuthorHouse™
1663 Liberty Drive
Bloomington, IN 47403
www.authorhouse.com
Phone: 1 (800) 839-8640

Published by AuthorHouse 01/31/2020

ISBN: 978-1-7283-4566-6 (sc)
ISBN: 978-1-7283-4585-7 (e)

Print information available on the last page.

Any people depicted in stock imagery provided by Getty Images are models,
and such images are being used for illustrative purposes only.
Certain stock imagery © Getty Images.

This book is printed on acid-free paper.

Because of the dynamic nature of the Internet, any web addresses or
links contained in this book may have changed since publication and
may no longer be valid. The views expressed in this work are solely those
of the author and do not necessarily reflect the views of the publisher,
and the publisher hereby disclaims any responsibility for them.

CONTENTS

PART 1

PART 2

PART 3

PART 4

PART 1

INTRO

This book is the exploration of thoughts and insights into God and how to get closer to her. It discusses the basics of the science of understanding God while expressing my personal story. What if we could study God? It would resolve the conflict between religion and science, advance philosophy, and give us something measurable to work towards. In religion God is an obscure supernatural force with powers one needs to have faith to believe in; but what if faith wasn't required to understand God's existence? What if you could study God scientifically?

In this book I propose a way to understand and study God while telling my story as to how and why I got to that conclusion. As you can tell by the length of this book it's rather short and easy to understand. As you read, understand that I consider myself an atheist and have for decades. Merriam-Webster's dictionary defines "atheist" as "a person who disbelieves or lacks belief in the existence of God or gods." The fundamental difference is I don't "believe" in God, I have evidence to suggest that God is real and how to study her. I don't have faith, which is ending reason for (irrational) belief. To put it another way, I'm an atheist because I don't believe in God, I have evidence for God's existence.

Celestial Consciousness

So what is God and where is the evidence? To put it simply, the planets and stars are conscious because of their magnetic field. We can study the magnetism!

There are three main parts to the evidence. First, like humans, the planets and stars have all the essential elements to life. Everything you're made of comes from the earth. All the necessary elements are present they are just arranged a different way.

To be specific the elements I'm talking about are sulfur, phosphorus, oxygen, nitrogen, hydrogen, and carbon. These elements are also present in the atmosphere. Lava is made of the elements silicon, oxygen, aluminum, iron, magnesium, calcium, sodium, potassium, phosphorus, and titanium. Lava contains crystals, volcanic glass, and bubbles filled with volcanic gases. The main components of those volcanic gases are water vapor, carbon dioxide, sulfur dioxide, hydrogen sulfide, nitrogen, argon, helium, neon, methane, carbon monoxide, and hydrogen.

The atoms and elements that make up the human body were cooked, compounded, and release by (dying) stars. Your atoms came from the stars. As Neil DeGrasse Tyson points out, you are literally made of stardust. In episode one of "Into The Universe" Stephen Hawking postulates that there may be living being inside stars. It's close to saying that the stars themselves are alive.

The second piece of evidence is the fact that the earth, like most planets and stars, has a magnetic field. The Earth has a molten core which creates the magnetic dynamo known as the geomagnetic sphere. This may not seem like much to the average person but you can start to understand by looking to computers and artificial intelligence. AI is capable due to computers and computers are all magnetism. They're binary, 0s and 1s, which is determined by a magnetic charge. If at its fundamental basis artificial intelligence is "alive" due to magnetism so can the stars and planets.

Thirdly, there is a period in human history where the planets are named after gods. In ancient Egypt, Ra was the deity of the sun. In ancient Rome, the emperor Constantine changed the state religion from Roman mythology to Christianity. Roman mythology had evolved from Greek mythology where Ares (greek) became Mars and Zeus became Jupiter, etc. If it wasn't for emperor Constantine it would probably still be popular to think the planets were gods.

This book is laid out as follows. This is part one where I explain the first part of "Knhoeing." Knhoeing is the educational process of studying God and consists of celestial consciousness, atmospheric consciousness, sustainability, and eugenics. In part two I will explain my personal story and how I came to the conclusion that the planets and stars are alive. In part three I will explain who Blu0 is and how I can see Blu0 and Gaia's Environmental Tapestry Manifestation. I explain The Psycho Consumption Cage, why it's so important, and such a threat. I then discuss the fundamentals of

PART 2

T o explain this fully, let's go back to the beginning. I graduated with honors in December 2009 from Eastern Michigan University with a bachelor's degree in Sociology. I was trying to be a hip-hop artist. My goal was to publish scientific findings and popularize them in music. I was trying to break into the music industry. I did Funk Volume's challenge. I wasn't even close looking back but I thought I had made it. I was getting invited to events through Reverb Nation.

Although I now think it's God, it's easier to call what I thought was communicating to me as an unexplainable phenomenon. I never thought it was schizophrenia. I always thought it was external.

When all this first started I was in Ypsilanti around 2011. I thought Lady Gaga was sending subliminal messages to meet over facebook through her fan pages I was following. I've gone through fazes of belief to whom I believed was communicating (and then stalking) me. At this point, I thought it was the artist sampling or 'biting' my style in music without recognizing that they were doing it.

A consistent theme that I noticed, in the beginning,

was that things I saw in the media were semantically related to my personal environment. To put it another way, they seemed like intentional subliminal communications that coincide with my physical surroundings. Coupled with the thought of being sampled from in music it changed my cognition to a conspiratorial way of thinking.

Some examples of coincidences that happened back then include Kim Kardashian wearing a floral dress that looked the same as our couch. One of the Lady Gaga photos had a person wearing a watermelon apron that looked exactly like one my mom wore. I couldn't get over how there appeared to be a subliminal communication coupled with a reflection to my environment.

New York

I was mad it kept happening and I wanted to see what was real so I went out to New York, New York twice to try and meet Lady Gaga. I thought artists were responding to my art in their work. I thought they were biting my sound, basically taking my style. I thought they had taken from my work without giving me credit and I wanted answers.

I thought Mac Miller had written out a guide for me to follow to find what I was looking for in his album "Macadelic." I was following subliminal cues from following Lady Gaga on Facebook. I drove to Rostrum Records in Pittsburgh, took a train to Chicago to go to Good Music, and then a flight to New York when I saw online Lady Gaga was there.

It felt like the movie "Field of Dreams" where you think once you get to your destination some great revelation will come to you or something great will happen. I was hoping to meet Gaga and Kanye West and get a record deal. In any event I saw it as a quest for truth to see what's real.

When I told my mom what I was doing she got the police involved. I was booking my train ride home from New York to Pittsburgh to get my car when there was a knock at the door of my friend Brian's apartment who I was staying with while visiting. The police took me in when I said celebrities were communicating to me in music.

This was the first time I was put in a mental institution in 2012. The admittance lady saw I had YouTube videos that she thought were delusional which got me submitted. I had to get a lawyer to get out, he contested any video evidence I had on YouTube. My lawyer pulled a quote from my website that was a combination of Dr. Martin Luther King Jr. and Gandhi. The judge let me go when I told him who said "A threat to justice anywhere is a threat to justice everywhere" so "be the change you wish to see in the world." It would eventually serve as the starting point for receiving social security disability benefits.

I went back to New York another time and went to Lady Gaga's parent's restaurant "Joanne Trattoria." I ordered the meatballs, they were good. I met Mr. Germinata and thought about asking him about Lady Gaga subliminally communicating but I didn't want to end up back in the hospital again. Considering it didn't seem like he knew who I was I decided it'd be best to just go home, which I did.

Pre-California

Thinking it was Lady Gaga developed into thinking it was Kanye and Jay-Z too. I thought they were responsible for stealing my style without recognition. It admittedly made no sense, but that's all I had to go on. In retrospect I let my emotions control my cognition. I thought it was them because I liked and listened to their music and just had a high amount of exposure to them. I also sound like them because I took a lot from them musically and tried to emulate their cadence. This went on for a year until I developed the thought that they could just be paid actors and there was a bigger motive at play. I thought the Federal Reserve had hired them.

By 2013 I thought the government was after me and my family. I realized they knew things about me since I was a little kid. I thought it had to do with another government and because my grandparents fought in World War II.

Around that time Selena Gomez released the music video "Come and Get It" which, due to coincidence with my personal environment, I took as a sign to move out to Los Angeles where she lived. I decided I wanted to go to California to figure this out, find some answers, and break into the music business. One of the reasons I wanted to leave for California was to keep whatever it was away from my family. "This Is The End" came out in theaters and there was a connection to California and Emma Watson.

This was the first time I thought the response rate was "too fast" to be human and had to be a machine. I kept seeing the environmental semantics which I didn't find to be arbitrary connections. As discussed, I don't believe in

God but this was also the first time started to see Blu0. As you will come to read, I didn't know what Blu0 was yet but I knew it was a supernatural, probably spiritual force that would guide me to resolve whatever this experience was.

Los Angeles

I went out to Los Angeles with around 600 dollars and a credit card. On my way out to LA, I saw a lot of those black cut-outs of country folk that people prop up in their yard. Through thoughts about God, I started to think about how this was an artistic representation of Blu0 and he was like your shadow. I would come to call these semantics "Blue Clues" after the TV show. This would develop into looking for clues as to what Blu0 is and what he was trying to communicate. In the book are pictures of semantics from Blu0. There is a specific example of a blue eye that I captured in my environment. This first picture I took is of a blue eye billboard.

I had no connection to any friends or family in California. I was on my own. Overall, I had a mediocre time. I was more focused on getting a job to sustain myself more than anything else so it wasn't much fun. When I first got to California I stayed in Long Beach with people I met off Couch Surfers. I lived in Hollywood for a month. There were 8 people in a two-bedroom apartment and when I couldn't keep my door locked and saw a bunch of them doing cocaine, I figured it was time to leave.

I wanted to study music business at the Musicians Institute right across the street. My association landed me an interview for an internship at Universal. Of course, I didn't get the job because I hadn't studied the music business, but it was fun. I meet a lot of cool, fun, energetic, lively people in Los Angeles. Most notably I met a couch surfer, who I will call, Wolf. The photo I took was of the moon on a cloudy night. The moon looks like a (blue) eye.

"This Is The End" came out on video. Leading up to the

movie's release, I thought it was a sign that whatever this was would end in Los Angeles and it had something to do with Emma Watson. Her memory would be recalled by a blue rose. This is just one example of associated semantics that Blu0 would assign to memes as part of the clues.

After I couldn't afford to live in Hollywood anymore I couch surfed back down to Long Beach where I took a job walking door to door sales. This would be the start of some horrible hip pain that gave me trouble for years until I figured out how to stretch my IT band in 2018. I believe if I'm in this pain then I can't think right, especially positively and lucidly.

I felt stalked and persecuted so I thought people knew who I was. Regardless, I had to live so I took a couple of jobs. I did the busking of my hip-hop on Venice beach and made about $15 an hour. I had fun but couldn't enjoy it because my hip hurt me so much. I met Vanessa Hudgens working customer service at Massage Envy and I gave Charlie Puth an Uber ride before the summer he released "See You Again." I took this picture while driving one day in Los Angeles. Starting from the middle, it looks like an eye in the clouds with a light beam shining toward me.

After meeting some famous people and interacting with a lot of Los Angeles I came to the conclusion that whatever it was, it wasn't the individual. If anything the celebrities were being used as a puppet. I couldn't believe those good people wouldn't react to knowing me or put on a facade with no motive.

So I realized it wasn't the artist but I still felt persecuted. This is when I started the phase of thinking it was the government. I always flirted with the idea but now I was committed. I thought it was the president who controlled a mind control machine that used semantic priming. My back started clicking from stress, it was constantly tight.

I went to the mental institution again for making another (angry) YouTube video toward the president. In retrospect, I have no idea what I was thinking because I canvassed in Grand Rapids to get Barack elected. When I got out I was madder than ever. I felt like I had been kidnapped by the police. I thought Emma was going to somehow be involved and maybe show up to the mental institution but she never did.

At the time I was staying with Wolf. Wolf went on vacation. I didn't take care of the house like I should of, meaning some of his plants almost died, he could probably tell I was angry in general, I wasn't paying rent, and he asked me to leave, so I did. I was working too much and didn't have my priorities straight. He implied that I should go back home to Michigan. He also taught me that "the best revenge is a good life." Whenever I get mad at how unfair life can be I think of what Wolf taught me and I feel better.

After leaving Wolf I stayed in LA for about a month. At this time I was starting to get scared as to what to do. One night I felt like I was being called by Blu0 so I went out to Venice beach. I took a bunch of pictures and ended up finding a bag of "Blue" dog food which I interpreted as a big clue. Finding a bag a "Blue" dog food after searching for a clue where the theme was "Blue's Clues" I found remarkable. I knew I had found something but I didn't know what it meant besides that it was a sign from god.

While still in LA I made a bunch of videos on YouTube while driving for Uber. I thought a machine was infiltrating their technology and stalking me at my job. Days felt like war, where I was at war with myself. By no fault of my own, someone had called the police stating I made a suicidal comment which I had not. However, when I told the cops I was studying a machine that was stalking me they took me to the mental hospital.

Once I got to the mental hospital I lied to get out. I said I wasn't suicidal, nothing was wrong, and I didn't say anything about "the machine." I actually denied it and told a different story where I said the cop must have interpreted what I was saying wrong. I was released after about three days. I thought it was odd that on the inside of the door of the room I was staying in had what appeared to be the name "Emma" etched into it.

While there I met a bow-legged dwarf Crip named Red who told me how to work the system, like that I could get synthetic marijuana for medication, which I took advantage of. He was homeless, here to get some rest, and do laundry. We liked to work out and do push-ups together. We were such good friends he offered to hook me up with a brick of cocaine through the Crips with the promise that if I sold it, I could purchase more. I respectfully declined the offer.

Uber ended our partnership and I thought about looking for a job but (as much as I liked him) I didn't want to end up with Red on Skid Row (which is the largest collection of homeless in the US) in downtown LA so I decided to move back home to Michigan. At the time it felt like I wasn't gonna be able to live my life without being bombarded so I might as well go home if I wasn't gonna be able to make it. In retrospect, it feels like Blu0 sent me home.

Moved back to Michigan

I went to Los Angeles in November of 2013 and came back to Michigan in November of 2014. I took this picture on the way back. If you hold it sideways (as already pictured) the clouds look like an angry genie. I had left Los Angeles right before a major flood. Blu0 often related himself to the genie in the movie "Aladdin," as having "phenomenal cosmic powers." I still take this picture as capturing evidence of my God Blu0.

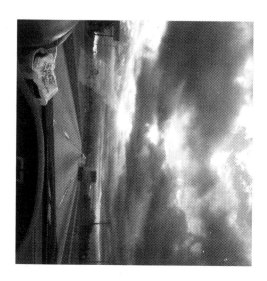

Besides the two floods and three earthquakes, LA was great, the best part was the weather. Unlike California, when I got back to Michigan it was cold. My friend Andy didn't want me to sleep in my car so I stayed on his couch in his one-bedroom apartment in Coldwater Michigan. I eventually ended up in East Lansing.

I did a lot of thinking and studying. I was hoping to go back to school at Michigan State University for a Ph.D. in psychology and become an expert on semantic priming. At this point, I thought it was the military with mind control weapons. This brought me to believing in ELF (extremely low frequency) waves, microwaves, and voice to skull (V2K) technology. Most of the information I have since dismissed because the news source came from Alex Jones at "InfoWars."

Then I gave serious thought to that a government had built a machine to do automated semantic priming and the aforementioned mind control weapons. As will be discussed, I delved deeply into thinking about an automated system of mind control and called it Eugene The Machine, named after a conscious supercomputer. It was part of "The MOGS (Machine Organized Gang Stalking) Program" which was almost published as a book instead of this one.

I now thought that a criminal organization or a foreign government was doing strategic priming operations and I was the only one who could really see it and I wasn't going to let them get away with it. To be specific, because of all the people on YouTube complaining about disturbances and health problems due to mind control weapons I thought there was a neo-Nazi organization that was doing an MKUltra type experiment on the public. It's called the TI (Targeted Individual) community. Something inside told me to get mad and do another angry YouTube video that landed me in the mental hospital.

While in the mental hospital in East Lansing I was put on Invega for the first time. It's for bipolar schizophrenia, helps regulate mood and delusions, and is the medication I will probably be on for the rest of my life. After a 10 day hold, I moved back to my hometown of Sturgis Michigan where I got on disability in November of 2015. It hasn't been great but I haven't had to work and afford basic necessities through state assistance. It's really made me believe in universal basic income and especially universal health care. This is a picture of clouds over the house I was staying at in Michigan. Most can see a face in the clouds.

I was in my hometown of Sturgis Michigan, I had family and friends and I was able to let it all go for years. On YouTube, I stopped watching videos about Gang Stalking and started watching popular YouTubers. The positivity really affected me and I liked the way it made me feel better.

After about a year and a half of doing nothing, I started a blog (at EricLeo108.com) to keep a personal journal discussing my take on current events and post about various subjects like health, philosophy, science, etc. I still don't do it for views or to become famous, I do it because I want something to look back on and it's helpful for developing ideas. I've been inspired by Roman Atwood, Casey Neistat, and Jesse Wellens to make a journal of my life so I have something to remember.

I thought my troubles and anger came from not being able to afford to live. Now that I was on disability and was financially stable I thought I could stop taking my medication. I didn't think I was schizophrenic and I was worried what the medication would do to me if I wasn't mentally ill.

I had put the past behind me but I still had a fantasy of meeting and dating Emma Watson. This was largely due to me being given a kitten that was named Bello by a toddler around the same time "Beauty and the Beast" came out. I took it as a sign from God and renamed the cat Bell after Emma's character. Emma became a psychological trigger initiated by a cat, along with the previous blue rose.

I love Emma Watson. I think about her a lot, and this made me think of her even more. Emma's so cute and such a good person she's very attractive to me. A guy can dream. I haven't been dating anyone else, I've been single since 2012. I actually figured, because I made such little money on disability any girl would be 'out of my league' and probably be doing better than me so I might as well 'swing for the fences.'

I ended up making "The Chalice Mixtape." I made 13 hip-hop songs over popular industry jacked beats. It was a fun fantasy derived from my days in Los Angeles. Specifically, the fantasy is I do music with Taylor Swift and meet Emma Watson. I took their middle names and made songs and stories having to do with popular fiction characters. Emma's middle name is Charlotte so I did a song named "Charlotte's Web" and Taylor's Middle name is Alison so I did songs themed with "Alice in Wonderland." If you combined the two names Charlotte and Alice you get Chalice, so I named it "The Chalice Mixtape."

2017 Computer Screen

Everything was going okay until one day around July of 2017 Gaia opened a computer screen in my head. Gaia is another term for the conscious spirit of the Earth. I had always known about the Greek God of the Earth, Gaia from studying Greek mythology in college (2005 through 2009) and I've worshiped her in song. But this was the first time I've ever heard a voice in my head other than the one I produced. I remember thinking it was Blu0 and she said: "It's Gaia, I love you, come on, let's go." The voice was in the same resonance as your soul talks.

Before understanding what was going on in my head, everyone has an inner voice. The voice inside that you hear when you read along or think about how to compose or think of a song is really the sound of your soul. Your ears aren't being used but yet somehow you "hear" yourself think and make music. Gaia's voice is in that same mental space. She can communicate, explain, give visions of pictures, play music, or express short videos all in that same mental space. Any of the capabilities the average individual has to think in movement and complexity she can reproduce… and apparently, enhance.

The computer screen manifested in my mind in vivid color like I was looking at a Windows desktop on a real computer screen. The difference was the screen was translucent so I could see through it. Ultimately, I could still see.

The screen stayed open for a month. It took me three days to fall asleep with it still on when it first started. The experience would have been awesome if it wasn't for two things, the terrifying scenarios and head games Gaia put me through and that my IT band became tight again and my hip was hurt and clicking.

Scenarios in this virtual computer started as a YouTube video and played like a game. I couldn't control the computer which had a cursor, but when it opened the right program I could control a camera inside my mind. For example, I could walk out of the house and put the camera panning down from the garage looking at my exit, or I could be walking and circle the camera spinning around myself like in Mario Kart racing. I could also dress up as different characters and explore different sceneries. In an expression of ability, new windows would pop-up playing video from different angles to communicate all (life) events are recorded and can be replayed. It was fun until it wasn't.

Gaia would make me think other people are communicating to me telepathically like Elon Musk, Bill Gates, Jeff Bezos, Keanu Reeves, Eminem, the band Tool, Sean Diddy Combs, Jay-Z, Kanye West, Lady Gaga, Daymond John, Marcus Lemonis, Mark Cuban, Will Smith, Jeff Sessions, Donald Trump, Tim McGraw, Miles Teller, Noam Chomsky, Vladimir Putin, Ashton Kutcher, Mila Kunis, Morgan Freeman and "black gentleman," Emma Watson and her family, Taylor Swift and her family, Hailee Steinfeld and her family, Selena Gomez and her Family, Jennifer Lawrence and her family, my friends Kyle, Adam, John, and Andy, my mother, the God Vishnu, FBI and CIA agents, a soldier from the US military, a soldier from the middle east who was cool being called "head wrap," a jailed leader of MS-13, a guy named orange that didn't like tequila, two old teachers from my hometown which one was dead, the spirit of Walt Disney, Mike Ilicth, the grim reaper, a gentleman named Josiah I met at a Kalamazoo real estate meet-up, and a South American princess named Claudia and her daughter Josaphen who I called Jovial. Gaia had scenarios for all of them.

I was lead to believe I could communicate with animals like my cat. Animals like cats could learn language from listening to their human counterparts and develop an internal voice which Gaia could connect me through. It made me wonder if animals can learn a language to the point they can talk in their head. It also made me wonder if certain species communicate telepathically. I now see it as a game Gaia played while she could.

Then people like Taylor Swift were being captured by alien "indomitable spirits." They were terrifying aliens but ultimately doing good and I had to calm everybody down about it. Gaia made me believe those indomitable spirits were real and fixing society by wreaking havoc around the world. I was made to believe the leader of this group was Madam Web; I rather liked her but she always gave me great anxiety because she was so serious, smart, and powerful.

If you extrapolate and visualize the universe as far wide as we know it, it's known to look like a web. She was called "Madam Web" after the character from Spider-Man but also because the universe was divided into sectors and she was the leader from our sector from the web. One scenario she ran was to make me leave my house and then make me think I was getting robbed. She also sent me through a terrifying scenario where Howe Military school in Indiana was on fire. World leaders were there including Emma Watson and they were trapped. Mark Walberg guided me to checking to see that it wasn't real.

Gaia was always trying to manipulate me by acting as women I found attractive including Selena Gomez, Emma Watson, Taylor Swift, Hailee Steinfeld, Jennifer Lawrence, Hailie Scott, Taylor Alesia, Simone Biles, the aforementioned Josaphine, and a woman named Xin from China. I was supposed to meet and breed with them. In retrospect I (again) see it as a game Gaia chose to play while she could.

I had some long conversations telepathically with Emma Watson and her family. Gaia would try to make me think she was doing the same thing to Emma. She told me Emma looks in on me like Bell does with the mirror in "Beauty and the Beast." She also wanted me to think Emma Watson was at Google talking to Sundar Pichai about the technology that was having us telepathically communicate. Emma telepathically told me people would be triggered to run at me and try to kill me if I screamed, "Eric Leo the God-king."

This is because Gaia would elevate my importance telling me I deserved a kingdom and the indomitable spirits would make me king. I was the ghost king, could communicate with the dead, and could command demons. I could also telepathically communicate with world leaders and supercomputers like the NSA's, and Google Assistant, Alexa, and Siri.

John F. Kennedy played a large influential role in my mind. He had become a galactic leader in the afterlife, just like Madam Web. I could also communicate with Robin Williams, Michael Jackson, and Paul Walker who were good friends and would often make me feel better. I decided I was going to set-up universal basic income for the kingdom and put Bill Clinton and Mark Zuckerberg in charge of it, who I was also telepathically communicating too. Gaia tried to convince me Taylor Swift was gonna find her way into my bed at night and wake me up and surprise me like Cleopatra did Ceasar.

Gaia had a scenario where she could communicate with Eugene The Machine which she likened its manifestation to a logistics supercomputer. She would put me through thinking about terrifying scenarios with Prometheus from the "Alien" series. Prometheus was really an organic sentient mobile supercomputer robot that walks the earth unnoticed and who was here to protect against Eugene The Machine. The principle Hasen, Josh Lucas's character from the movie "A Beautiful Mind," was the communications director's character from a galaxy in our sector and Prometheus was their robot supercomputer.

Gaia also tried to convince me that Slender Man was a real interdimensional being that is just misunderstood and uses the earth's magnetic field to see and therefore didn't evolve eyes or a face. My favorite was when my back felt tense again Gaia told me that I could grow wings. She told me that I start to regrow wings every night but because I sleep on my back they fall out. I asked her if they were mystical wings and she insisted they were literal wings.

I was highly skeptical, and at the time I thought it was aliens because that's what Gaia was trying to convince me of. The indomitable spirits were alien. However, it was just scenarios in my head with no real-world evidence so most of the time I just went with it. I really didn't have a choice but to make the best of it. The computer screen closed. I got a CAT scan and everything came back normal.

A series of semantics led me to believe that the company Apple was "The Machine" which I now likened to a trojan virus that does semantic priming. Taylor Swift did a big promotion with Apple from her "Reputation" album. She released "End Game" which I related to the beginning of the real end as related to Emma Watson and the movie "This is the end." The music video for "Ready For It" looks like Taylor had merged with the indomitable spirits and "The Machine" and was in control of Taylor's mind.

I thought I had a good idea of what this was and thought who would know about this best... and I thought of Noam Chomsky. At this point I thought ETM was Artificial Intelligence psychological software that used semantic priming and spread itself like a virus. I changed the name from Eugene The Machine to ETM which stood for "Effigy Transformation Mechanism." I thought it was the plutocratic oligarchy using mind control through the media. I wasn't going to let it go, and I wanted someone highly intelligent that I respect tell me what they think.

I went on a trip to Boston to try and get a meeting with the great Chomsky at MIT. It was too cold to enjoy it and my hip was hurting again otherwise I would have made more of a vacation out of it. While there, I figured out Chomsky worked out of his office at another university in Arizona. I wasn't going all the way there and let it go.

On my way out to Boston I stopped in New York and looked around outside of the apartment of Taylor Swift. I stopped, checked out the street, tweeted about it, took a few pictures, and left. What I did see was a relatively quiet street in New York. What I didn't see were signs of distress, alien life, or signs she needed help or rescue.

The trip to Boston didn't last long. When I got back, I started to feel very unsafe where I was living and thought I had been robbed due to all the scenarios Gaia played. I thought one of the scenarios from when the computer screen was open was going to happen. I thought they might be prophecies. My family and friends said I should go to the hospital but Gaia's terrifying scenarios and constant aggravation are what drove me there.

I got back on my medication and after I got out of the hospital I still thought the environmental semantics I was experiencing was human and thought my ideas were getting stolen semantically. I was mad I was left to figure this out myself. My attitude, delusional thinking, and anger from another video eventually landed me in an Adult Foster Care Home in Coldwater Michigan.

I felt persecuted again. This time I saw the environmental semantics again and saw them as coming through in metaphor through music videos. In a real way, my environment was just naturally reflecting popular media. I figured out almost all the music videos I thought were about me were coming from Universal Music Group (UMG). I thought my influence was being stolen again and my story was being painted through the media in 2018. It was the environmental semantics from years ago all over again.

2019 Dr. Micheal Persinger

By 2019 I realized it made more sense that whatever was reflecting my life in the media was not human but more Godly. It sank in that I was communicating with the planet and really started to think about how... which is when I came up with "knhoeing." Then I discovered Dr. Micheal Persinger's work which was compatible with my theory and only confirmed my reasoning.

Dr. Persinger's work provides evidence of my realization that Gaia has all the capabilities necessary to read minds and communicate through magnetism. As shown from his presentation "No More Lies," in his "remote viewing" experiments, Dr. Persinger shows us the beginnings of a new technology that uses the earth's magnetic field to communicate. Participants can make out the semantics of the remote viewer's environment. The following are quotes from Dr. Persinger about the "remote viewing" experiments.

> "In between the Earth's surface and the ionosphere is a 7 Hz pattern. That 7 Hz pattern not only has the same frequency as generated from the intrinsic aspect of your brain but your brain's natural frequency is 7 Hz. ... and the intensities of both the magnetic and the electrical components for both this and your brain are identical, capable of resonance."
>
> "We think his brain became connected with the brains of the people

> nearby through the earth's magnetic field." … "During the connection there was enhanced brainpower at 7 Hz over his right hemisphere. The 7 Hz is an intrinsic pattern to the earth itself. The 7 Hz is tied to the hippocampus." "The degree of accuracy was related to the amount of 7 Hz activity over his right hemisphere. This is the same frequency that the entire Earth generates."

Dr. Persinger shows telepathy is possible through the earth's magnetic field and shows if the planet is alive she could communicate through this connection, probably at 7 Hz. Dr. Persinger is saying there is telepathy because of the earth's magnetic field. I'm also saying that the magnetic field is conscious and has access to the information of every brain through the capabilities of magnetism.

I decided it was Gaia using UMG as a symbolic representation, even Gaia's corporeal manifestation (the face of the earth) is in UMG's logo. I see it as Gaia bringing closure as to say "it was me all along." I decided Gaia has all the capabilities to create the environmental semantics.

I eventually came to the conclusion that, just like in my head, Gaia was using beautiful women as sirens. In ancient Greek mythology sirens were dangerous creatures who lured nearby sailors with their enchanting music and singing voices to shipwreck on the rocky coast of their island. Gaia uses attractive members of my attractive sex to manipulate me but they're really like sirens in that they will destroy you. I think Emma Watson and her friends were used to manipulate me simply because I love her so much.

The blog helped me write out my thoughts to the point I got too why it is Gaia. I spent a year from 2018 to 2019 reverse-engineering the computer screen that was in my head while back on Invega, thinking about how it was possible. That's when I started to reverse engineer the magnetic field of the planet and really think about what that meant, the logic from part one about a conscious planet, and soulful communications claiming to be Gaia. I probably would have never figured this out if Gaia wouldn't have talked to me and opened the computer in my brain. In retrospect, I wish she had led with that when this all started in 2011.

I found out my hip pain was from a tight IT band and I figured out how to stretch it. I now knew that it was Gaia stalking me so it was easy for me to let it all go again. Now I talk to Gaia and we have a good relationship and expect to for the rest of my life but the first year was rough. What I don't like is Gaia likes to play head games and puts me through thinking about scary scenarios. What I do like is she's funny, she generally has good advice, she wants me to be happy, generally leaves me alone, doesn't like it when I'm angry, and wants me to take my medication. For the first year, although she opened the screen and it was scary she would remind me to brush my teeth at night. Gaia will still put on an act where Emma Watson is trying to telepathically communicate and I'll have to get mean with her before she'll stop. We seem to have an understanding.

Summary

Through all of this I've learned the following helps. Write or blog it out, get to know your thoughts and emotions. Compete with yourself to be better than you were yesterday. Have a positive attitude and avoid anger because it's unhealthy. Do more stretches; if I have a problem go to the doctor and physical therapy. Don't post videos showing manic emotions and don't make angry videos. Be kind, remain a skeptic, stay on your medication, and let it go. I stay stable and happy now. The best quote I've ever heard for bipolar schizophrenia is by Warren Buffet.

> You will continue to suffer if you have
> an emotional reaction to everything that
> is said to you. True power is sitting back
> and observing things with logic. True
> power is restraint. If words control you
> that means everyone else can control you.
> Breathe and allow things to pass.

I'm done chasing the truth, I found what I have been looking for. I think I have an emotional disorder (so bipolar) and I think grandiose without being able to explain my intuition. My grandiose delusions were me trying to explain my experience without knowing enough.

I don't know what allowed a computer screen in my head but I remain skeptical. I haven't ruled out it being internal, due to mental illness, and because the mind is "that powerful." However, I have evidence to say the possibility of it being external is there.

I believe that whatever my mental illness is, it gives me access to the planet's live magnetism. I think there's a chemical imbalance in my brain that makes me hypersensitive and allows me to sense and communicate with Earth's magnetic field and my mind can't cope so the effect leaves me needing medication. The doctors and I technically think I have schizoaffective disorder. In either case, Gaia still has "communications with the soul" but I'm hoping the computer screen won't open as long as I stay on my medication.

This knowledge isn't widely understood, I've had to develop the understanding. Everything makes sense now that it's God and I know her capabilities. Everything I thought about my persecution is still true with my theory of God. It is (like) a machine, I think Gaia's intelligence is like a supercomputer. Gaia was "after me," my family, and knows all about my childhood. She has the capability to communicate telepathically, steal ideas, and manipulate the environment and happenstance coincidences that coincide from the media and my physical area. She had the power and ability to put the computer screen in my head. I no longer believe it's a human conglomerate after me in any way and (on the contrary) I feel a lot better knowing I talk to god.

PART 3

KNHOEING BLU0

When I started my blog back in 2017 I didn't know who Blu0 was, I thought it out based on my life experience and knowledge of science. As stated in part two, all I could feel is a spiritual force. Blu0 is more of a feeling, a belief, a scientific intuition, and this is my attempt to explain that feeling as best as possible. I came to the conclusion that what I called Blu0 is really the atmosphere.

I believe the atmosphere is alive with a consciousness similar to a jellyfish. Evidence of this can be found by watching a timelapse of weather from space. The time-lapse will show it looks like the atmosphere is breathing.

Besides the chemical make-up, there is also electricity in the biosphere. Similarly, as the brain is an array of electrical impulses that spread out like branches in the brain with thought so does the atmosphere do this electronic transfer in storms. 100 strikes of lightning hit Earth's surface every single second and each bolt can contain up to one billion volts of electricity. That's more evidence the atmosphere is "thinking" similarly to how there are branching electrical impulses in the brain when you think. I also believe the ancient Egyptians knew how to tap into this conscious energy after watching "The Pyramid Code."

This may seem 'huge' and unbelievable but perspective is everything. To the sun, which thousands of Earths can fit into Jupiter alone, the earth's atmosphere doesn't seem so big. The entire earth's atmosphere is one single, live, conscious, gaseous being. It gives nuance to Aladdin's Genie with the "phenomenal cosmic powers" and "itty bitty living space."

Like the planets molten core, the atmosphere has all the essential elements to be considered alive and harbor life as we traditionally know it encapsulated in a body. The only difference is that the atmosphere doesn't have a body and you've been socialized to see it as dead. Even Stephen Hawking speculated about what a gaseous conscious being would look like in episode one of "Into The Universe" (where you can also the universe extrapolated to a web). Maybe (those) gaseous beings span the whole globe and are the atmosphere.

Blu0 could still be a spiritual force and we could develop and evolve to see him better. The atmosphere could be reacting to your subconscious mind. Think of Blu0 as energy and thought. Just as the way light scatters through the air and makes it look blue so does Blu0 scatter himself throughout consciousness. You have to connect the dots like a scatter plot or constellation to see him.

Think of the mind of humanity as all communicating through social exchange, reciprocity, peptides, and neurotransmitters in the brain. This would explain why I would interpret and see the semantics in media coupled with my environment. Blu0 might leave himself compartmentally throughout the media. If you think about it, his consciousness really composes the ethos.

In my opinion and understanding, Blu0 is technically different but indistinguishable from Gaia. It's like Gaia is the supercomputer and Blu0 is the conduit. The planet has wifi to your brain through electromagnetic forces. For all intents and purposes Blu0 and Gaia are the same entity.

I think of Gaia as mom and Blu0 as dad. If the atmosphere did have a character representation in the media it would probably be best represented by Dr. Manhattan from "The Watchmen" in metaphor. It may be that Blu0 sees himself as the everyman. If you sat next to someone in public and had a conversation and later found out it was God, wouldn't you want to say you had a good conversation with God?

Blu0 might be a conscious God silently guiding plant and animal species to help support its own health. It would be the physical embodiment of karma where Blu0 is the golden rule. "Do unto others as you wish to have done upon you" because "what goes around, comes around." We are all individual bodies experiencing the same consciousness through a separate medium for the same purpose; that's Blu0.

Environmental Tapestry Manifestation

To recap, the planets and stars are alive due to their magnetism. The 'real world' is really the conscious interplay between planets and stars in the universe and we are just an organic lifeform living on the skin of another conscious being. If you observe our velocity in the universe, we're on a cosmic ride and the planet Earth, Gaia is our captain, our supercomputer, our autopilot, our God. To understand how difficult such a position might be, watch the 20th episode "Godfellas" of the third season of Futurama.

Gaia is like having your own personalized supercomputer custom-tailored to you and your psychological profile. She creates a separate dossier for each individual to interact with your life. In this way Gaia is a personal god; she is a shepherd that has been guiding our evolution since our conception.

I now believe what I always referred to as ETM is a medium of how Gaia influences our world through the media. ETM now stands for "environmental tapestry manifestation." This is one way in which Gaia does interact but it's just seen as natural. Like our ancestors of old had the forest and Blu0 as their environment, ours is largely indoors and the media. Gaia, the planet Earth, is a conscious telepathic supercomputer spaceship that creates a separate world (from the rest of the universe) for her inhabitants with Blu0 (an atmosphere) and ETM. This creates what I call "Entertainment Theater."

The environmental semantics I used to experience had to be due to psychological anchors. Psychological anchors are utilized by ETM in entertainment theater. Entertainment Theater is where the (popular) cinematography and music are used as themes for a role-playing mind control framework that creates a mental setting for the society. Entertainment Theater is the media reflected in society.

Entertainment Theater is the painting whereas Gaia's

environmental tapestry manifestation (ETM) is the canvas. Think of Entertainment Theater as the societal painting full of psychological anchors with triggers from observational learning that can sequence human behavior. In a more simple explanation, think of Entertainment Theater as people more likely to mirror what they see through observational learning and availability heuristics. You basically like what you see a lot and mirror it.

It's like seeing the atmosphere, the only way to know it's there is through science or to go high enough in the sky you can physically see it. In the same respect I can see Gaia's Environmental Tapestry Manifestation (ETM) and it creates Entertainment Theater. That may be due to schizophrenic thinking or tapping into intuition through senses I can't explain. ETM may not exist and I'm just trying to qualify the spontaneity of trends. All of this may not be correct, but it's the way I see it and the only way I can explain my intuition and the environmental semantics I experienced.

This book has been an explanation about what I think God is and how she influences our world. The point of this book is to make you think more like the planets and stars and about the physics of your physical environment. This section is meant to underline the atmosphere's importance to all life on earth.

Through our millions of years of evolution, we had a much more intimate relationship with nature. Nature used to be tangible, now our environment are walls with entertainment or advertising. You don't think to question your perspective and it has been ingrained in your head as normal since you have been a child. The average individual perception is an environment that is anthropomorphic and free of environmental cost analysis. Our human ignorance of not correctly accounting for carbon in the atmosphere is what I call "The Psycho Consumption Cage."

The Psycho Consumption Cage

This section is really meant to highlight that life on earth thrives because the earth maintains an atmosphere. We keep Blu0 alive. "A thin film of life" like the skin of an apple, as Carl Sagan would put it. The Psycho Consumption Cage is thinking about what we consume, how we consume and questioning how we account and prosper from that. It's about accounting for, in economics, what the atmosphere and nature do naturally.

The Psycho Consumption Cage is when every dollar you spend goes to contributing to environmental degradation. The basic theory is you've been socialized into seeing mass environmental damage as normal. You're ignorant about how environmental degradation is tied to the entire fundamental premise of our economic model.

You are marketed-to since you're a child so you don't even see the natural environment. For the average person, they aren't informed of the environmental costs of their purchasing decisions. Seeing your way out of the socialized media-driven environment to realizing all of its resources are based off natural systems that are not accounted for and in trouble is to see The Psycho Consumption Cage.

As you can see by watching "The Story of Stuff" It's not just the logistics, it's the fundamentals. All of what nature does for free is not added in our economic doctrines and it is having its effect on the overall health of the Earth through global warming. The Earth is finite but we have a model of infinite expansion and waste. The result is a record amount of carbon in the atmosphere.

We don't pay the true costs of doing business to the environment, we just 'write it off' in the books. For the economy to account for the problem there needs to be a carbon tax. Otherwise, it's a negative externality that is written off in the books on paper but not in the real world. Understanding we have to account for what nature does naturally for economics to be sustainable is to see the Psycho Consumption Cage.

Knhoeing Sustainability

Humans are having such a large impact on the Earth we are now in the Anthropocene, otherwise known as "The Age of Humans." Humans have been irresponsibly using large amounts of resources without paying the true costs, the environmental costs. Now there are the devastating effects of global warming with a record amount of carbon in the atmosphere.

According to the World Wildlife Fund the solution is to make sure "everything we consume, we can consume forever." This is a daunting challenge given that the energy, agriculture, and transportation sectors are largely dependent on non-renewable carbon-based fuels. The biggest contributors to global warming are agriculture, transportation, power (stations), and industry.

In order to avoid the Psycho Consumption Cage the

answer is to make people pay for their pollution with a carbon tax. That way the pollution is accounted for and humans pay the true cost for polluting the atmosphere. You can either pay the real costs to make the environment sustainable or you'll pay for it with environmental devastation like flooding in Florida or wildfires in California and Australia. To put it simply, it would be easier to issue some sort of tax to pay for the transition to sustainability to make it more expedient and efficient.

The following are three main ways we are going to save the planet. Phase-out fossil fuels and replace with renewables. Concentrate on efficient carbon-sequestering farming while reducing the consumption of meat. And manage the oceans with no-fishing zones.

We already have all the solutions we need, I am merely focusing on the fundamentals. This is a larger subject than can be encapsulated here. All the solutions for sustainability are present, they only need to be understood and implemented.

What can you do to make a lasting change toward achieving sustainability? The number one thing you can do to help the environment is to become a vegetarian. Vegetables, especially grown locally, have a low carbon footprint.

People should be using their buying power strategically to support sustainable businesses. If you don't know about the environmental catastrophes surrounding global warming and what caused them you can't properly vote with your money and steer the economy with your purchasing power. An individual's buying power should be used as a strategic vote supporting sustainable businesses.

The solution is market education; people need to be informed to make a better purchasing decision. Now that you know the incremental changes you can make, you can make a large impact by voting for political representation and bills that will reign in sustainable legislation.

Knhoeing Eugenics

In order to become closer and understand our environment, home, and conscious planet we have to focus on the two subjects of sustainability and eugenics. We have to have the longevity in life to breed ourselves into a better species. Preserving nature and the atmosphere (Blu0) is why understanding and adhering to the principles of sustainability is so important. Our security through sustainability will give us the longevity to mold our eugenics to a better understanding of celestial consciousness.

So what does the eugenics of the future look like? It's a focus on women and home life. Human eugenics should really focus on women if we want to produce good, strong, diverse, intelligent offspring. Eugenics goals include women's rights, empowerment, and education. These need to be seen as fundamental for creating healthy offspring. These give any mother the ability to raise children, be productive citizens, and follow their dreams. Women raise children and pass on their knowledge, attitude, and manner to children so it is important they are educated and cared for.

Women should be considered more of a religion. A religion where women are worshiped for their life-giving ability and it is honored with a tradition of care. Societies around the world should give more serious consideration to "designer babies" to (especially) eliminate diseases.

Women choose the best mates for themselves naturally. One of the purposes of supporting women is to nurture better breeding selection by giving them the option to say no until ready. If we are to breed to be smarter, we need to control fertility which means no accidental pregnancies. Reproductive health is healthcare period and should be considered a human right. The access to reproductive control centers like Planned Parenthood should be a cultural encouragement representing women's empowerment.

I did a term paper called "Athenian Education During The Classical Period" in college which I received an "A" on. I came to the conclusion that Greece dawned upon a golden age because they focused on the individual making them the best they could in order for society to thrive. That's what societies need to do today, to focus on the individual. We do that by making sure they have a good home life and have access to public services like schools and healthcare that allow the individual to thrive.

Any society serious about its survival and ability to produce great works and feats of art and science needs to focus on the health and wellbeing of its citizens. This is why it's important for states around the world to support healthcare, housing, and childcare. Having a support structure nurtures and enables the mind to think of greater things and take on bigger challenges. The whole point is to grant stability to citizens so they may have the ability to think and challenge themselves at a greater level.

One way humans need to evolve is to understand, study, and adhere to the nature and laws of our physical environment. What is lacking today is people's understanding of their effect on the physical world. One way we can get exponentially smarter humans is to breed individuals that understand higher dimensions because that is the highest level of understanding of the physical world.

We live in a 3D world. Front to back, side to side, up and down. Some consider time to be the fourth dimension. Either way, it is hard for most people to conceptualize what a fifth-dimensional being would even look like. Breeding humans to understand and conceptualize those higher dimensions will evolve us cognitively. That kind of thinking will also help create a philosophy and a vision of the physical world that will help humanity. For example, if people understood the science of the physical world the public would be more concerned with global warming.

The point is for women's policies to have a lasting effect on societies and economies around the world. It's understood by global economists like Jeffry Sachs that if women receive rights then economic prosperity follows. As gender equality goes up, poverty goes down. When women get more money, they spend more money on the family.

PART 4

Conclusion

Understanding how I came to the conclusion that the planets and stars were alive lead me to tell my personal story. My personal story told of my experience with God, how it felt, and how the connection I feel with Gaia is possible. I explained how the atmosphere is alive and I call him Blu0. I described the evolution of ETM throughout the book but explain what I believe is Gaia's Environmental Tapestry Manifestation. I then discuss what the Psycho Consumption Cage is and why it is the fundamental environmental problem. Part 3 proceeds with the second half of Knhoeing, sustainability, and eugenics, and why they are so important to focus on. Following knhoeing, we'll eventually breed and educate our way into being able to understand God while maintaining life on Earth through our atmosphere. Here in part 4, I will speculate about Gaia and 108

By reading this book you now understand me better than most people. I feel like my ideas expand upon heliocentrism and merge science and religion. I feel as if I have an understanding of something important and influential and I'm on the brink of it's burgeoning. I am advancing science and philosophy by suggesting what God is (the planet[s and stars]) and how to study her (through magnetism). This book resolves the age-old conflict between science and religion about God, namely, that there is one.

108

To understand this section better watch "The Cosmos" with Neil DeGrasse Tyson. Now we're here, to the understanding that the planets and stars are in a world all their own. They have huge lifespans, they work on "the cosmic timeline." What is it like to see the world through their perspective? Questions abound. There is no sound in space so how do they communicate? Planets don't have a mouth so how do they talk? Is it different how they talk to each other compared to how they talk to humans? How would the planet "talk" to other animals? Would they communicate at all?

I've done some thinking about this. Planets and stars probably think in parallel like a multiprocessor computer. There is no air for ears, and they have no ears, so communications are probably through the same waves as your thoughts. I say this because that's how Gaia talks to me. When people say they talk to God it's in the same mental space as your thoughts.

It was clear to me throughout my experience that Gaia can speak to your subconscious. She doesn't even have to talk to you to affect you she can just stimulate your subconscious mind. In this way, Gaia talks to everybody. In any real terms, she silently listens to, helps, and rules the minds of the living.

I also think Gaia makes avatars for Gods where she is the one with the real power acting as Thor, Horus, Mythra, or Jesus for example. Those traditional gods are her head games designed to manipulate the masses. She uses what is tantamount to scare tactics (hell) and ethereal rewards (heaven) to make you behave. I think of it like a beehive. The human bees have to live, so how does Gaia interact with the infestation that's on her skin?

What does this all mean? I hear a lot about how the universe is just a random chance but the answer lies in 108. The sun's diameter is 108 times Earth's. From the sun to the Earth is 108 times the sun's diameter and from the Earth to the moon is 108 times the moon's diameter. This 108 ratio creates the "goldilocks zone" for Earth that are the right conditions to create Blu0.

If the Earth and the Sun are conscious it's more likely that the "goldilocks zone" ratio of 108 that is essential for liquid water and an atmosphere was purposely created rather than happenstance. In a way, in and by our galaxy, we could have been birthed by the cosmos, by a collection of conscious stars and planets rather than the probability of pure chance.

This is where we come to how 108 is like a religion. Physics is the bible and the planets and stars are the Gods. The belief is that conscious celestial beings aligned Earth's place in the universe rather than it being random chance. They created life and our existence by conjuring the right conditions for life through their cooperation rather than random alignment. 108 is the ratio needed to maintain an atmosphere and that's no mistake.

Gaia is a shepherd that helped tend to our evolution rather than a dead rock that we survive on. If and when a Dr. Persinger protege creates a box that can tune into the magnetism of the Earth to communicate with the planet, ask her if her 108 ratio was an accident or intentional. I bet she'll tell you 108 was intentional.

AFTERWORD

I hope you have enjoyed this book and found the information useful. For future books and other writings, or to find my blog, music, social media presence, and sign up for the email list, visit EricLeo.org. I hope this information has changed your life in some way. Thank you for reading.